Whatever happened to the peace process?

Report of a public debate organised by

Springfield Inter-Community Development Project

Published February 2002 by Island Publications
132 Serpentine Road, Newtownabbey, Co Antrim BT36 7JQ

ISBN 1 899510 33 8

Farset Community Think Tanks Project is funded by
The European Special Support Programme for Peace and Reconciliation

The public debate upon which this pamphlet is based was held on
1 November 2001 at the **Belfast Unemployed Resource Centre**

The organisers of the debate
Springfield Inter-Community Development Project
wish to thank the following speakers for their contributions:

Brian Feeney (political columnist)
Roy Garland (author/columnist)
Jim Gibney (Sinn Féin)
Barbara McCabe, *chair* (Ulster People's College)
Dr Beverly Milton-Edwards (Queen's University)
Dr Pete Shirlow (University of Ulster)

Printed by Regency Press, Belfast

Introduction

The Northern Ireland 'peace process' has experienced its share of ups and downs. Sometimes it seemed on the verge of collapse, at other times politicians were lauding (yet another) 'historic breakthrough'. Furthermore, there has always been confusion as to just what this 'peace process' is all about. Is it something owned exclusively by the Northern Ireland political parties, the British and Irish governments, and the host of British, Irish and Northern Irish civil servants? Or is it something much broader, something which embraces all of Northern Ireland's deeply divided communities?

In April 2001 Springfield Inter-Community Development Project had organised a public debate on the theme: 'Citizenship in a modern society' (published as Island Pamphlet No. 41). That debate revealed the rich diversity of perspectives from which the concept of citizenship could be addressed. Subsequent to that event SICDP received requests to facilitate a similar public debate on the equally pertinent theme: 'Whatever happened to the peace process?' That debate took place on 1 November 2001, at a time when the 'peace process' in *both* its manifestations – party political and inter-communal – was under intense strain.

On the political level David Trimble and his Ulster Unionist Party had collapsed the power-sharing Executive because of lack of progress on the decommissioning of IRA weapons. As the crisis deepened the IRA leadership made an 'historic gesture' by agreeing to put a quantity of weapons and ammunition 'beyond use'. Trimble felt sufficiently encouraged by this gesture to recommend that his party retake their seats on the Executive. However, having resigned as First Minister he now had to seek re-election, and two dissident members of his party were preparing to vote against such an outcome. The SICDP public debate took place the day before that crucial vote was due to be taken.

As for the inter-communal 'peace process': a summer of intense rioting in North Belfast – the worst for many years – had been followed by a bitter inter-communal stand-off at Holy Cross Primary School where Catholic schoolgirls and their parents faced a daily protest from Protestant residents, who in turn were attempting to draw attention to numerous grievances of their own community.

Such destabilising events, whether political or communal, only serve to confirm that the 'peace process' – however we define it – is fragile, and will require the efforts of everyone in this society if it is to succeed. The very least that must happen is for debate and dialogue between our communities to be pursed with a new urgency.

Séamus Colligan *Springfield Inter-Community Development Project*
Michael Hall *Farset Community Think Tanks Project*

Whatever happened to the peace process?

Barbara McCabe I have been asked to chair this evening's conference entitled 'Whatever happened to the peace process?' We have a range of speakers who I'll just introduce briefly before we hear from each of them. Roy Garland is a member of the Ulster Unionist Party and a columnist with the *Irish News*. Jim Gibney is a member of Sinn Féin's Ard Comhairle and Director of Political Campaigns. Brian Feeney is a journalist, commentator and historian. Pete Shirlow is a lecturer in Geography at the University of Ulster. Beverely-Milton Edwards is a lecturer in Middle-East Politics and Ethnic Conflict at Queen's University, and author of *Contemporary Politics in the Middle East*.

Roy Garland

Thank you very much for the invite. The question 'Whatever happened to the peace process?' seems to be based on the assumption that the peace process is on its last legs, or is entirely dead. But there is a difference between the peace process and the present political arrangements – the Assembly and all the rest of it – which are potentially in difficulties at the moment. In my view the peace process is not finished, and in light of last week's putting of weapons beyond use by the IRA, I wonder if the question is still appropriate. It is similar to another question which I have heard in some communities: what has the peace process given us, what have we got out of it? And in response to that I would say: ask not what the peace process can do for me, but what I can do for the peace process. I think there is a need for people to shoulder responsibility, because the peace process is wider than the political process and politicians – everyone has a responsibility within it.

We always knew it wouldn't be easy, we knew that overcoming the past and creating a new future was a long-term project in which we would face serious obstacles. We knew that overcoming sectarianism, vested interests, fear, ignorance, rivalry and malevolence would cause the fainthearted to question, if not to stumble. Despite all the fits and starts the peace train, I believe, is moving towards its destination, and the destination is a normal society and all that that entails, and hopefully one with greater tolerance, freedom, justice and equality. When the IRA initiated actual decommissioning last week this undoubtedly constituted an historic development and removed a major obstacle. Nor should David Trimble's contribution be minimised or underestimated. Like most Unionist leaders he has faced the intrigues of ambitious opponents. Unlike Terrence

O'Neill, however, his opponents have so far been unable, in any literal sense at least, to 'bomb' him out of office, as O'Neill was bombed out of office.

Instead he has faced the wrath of so-called traditional Unionists – which too often means sectarian Unionists – who have ranted and intimidated. Even outside his own home carloads of people have arrived up to protest, and that's not well known. In my view the spotlight should not be so much on the difficulties in the peace process, but rather at the *source* of those difficulties.

Dissidents, Republican or Unionist, in my view offer us the same package: an intensification of sectarian animosity and conflict. They have no vision, no strategy and no hope. Ian Paisley, in an article in last night's *Belfast Telegraph*, asks Unionists to consider whether they are better off now than four years ago. The question is: why did he not ask us to consider if we are better off now than during the thirty years of conflict? I think that says something about what he is thinking in his own mind – that, in fact, things *are* better. Paisley knows, if he has considered the nature of Republicanism at all, that irrespective of the amount of weapons involved, *any* move by the IRA on this issue is of major significance. But we must not be taken in by Paisley's rhetoric. If John de Chastelain* was as unreliable as Paisley suggests he is he could have conned us into believing that decommissioning had happened months ago. The DUP dismissal is disingenuous, represents bad faith and sour grapes. The start of IRA decommissioning has vindicated the stand of David Trimble, as it has vindicated the stand of other pro-Agreement Unionists and Nationalists. Like all political dinosaurs, however, the DUP and their dissident Republican fellow-travellers will sooner or later face the fate that awaits prehistoric animals who prove unable to change.

Dissidents, Republican or Unionist, in my view offer us the same package: an intensification of sectarian animosity and conflict. They have no vision, no strategy and no hope.

The peace process is based on lofty, inclusive and humanitarian ideals, and offers us something which we never had: an inclusive, democratic society at peace with itself and with its neighbours. It represents an attempt to reform society in the absence of victory for any side. The project *is* political, but it goes far beyond the bartering and compromise which typifies any political process. It involves making peace with former enemies, in a context where deep hurts and suspicions can be exploited by the unscrupulous. Peace makers, particularly those involved in the political arena, place themselves in danger, because in order to secure peace they must occasionally step out beyond the realms of acceptability within their constituencies.

The old political mould must be broken. In pursuit of this Ulster Unionists have taken risks, Republicans have taken risks, the SDLP have taken risks,

* The Canadian general leading the Independent International Commission on Decommissioning, tasked with overseeing weapons decommissioning as part of the Good Friday Agreement.

Loyalists have taken risks, even the Women's Coalition and the Alliance Party have taken risks. What risks have the DUP taken? They have chosen to reap the benefits without paying the price. They rest in regal splendour in the Assembly while pretending that this is some kind of mystical illusion. As for anti-Agreement Republicans and Loyalists, in my view they offer us nothing but sorrow, heartbreak, suffering and death. Sectarianism flaunts its ugly head and has the potential to delay, but not to stop, progress. It thrives on hurts and fears that are renewed on a daily basis by further acts of sectarian terrorism. At times the cancer appears to be in remission, but it has not been cured. It can lie silently like some dormant biological poison until it breaks out in subtle and discreet ways that are difficult to detect. At other times there are intense eruptions that are contagious and which infect other parts of the body politic.

For many dissidents the stimulation of this poison has become almost an art form. Ian Paisley never comments on our failure to decommission sectarianism. Nor has he apologised or offered apology for the cynical way sectarianism has been exploited by politicians for political advantage down the years. Responsibility lies particularly upon those within leadership, but leaders cannot lead without backroom boys. We have got to initiate dialogue across the divide in all kinds of ways. Bigotry, intolerance and misunderstanding can only be countered through direct contact. Occasionally bigger steps are possible and major advances can be made. But these are fraught with difficulties so long as sectarianism remains a virulent cancer to be fostered by those who reject progress.

[Sectarianism] can lie silently like some dormant biological poison until it breaks out in subtle and discreet ways that are difficult to detect. At other times there are intense eruptions that are contagious and which infect other parts of the body politic.

Politicians are often caught between the need to open doors to their opponents and the necessity to keep their own people on board. In this sense we are deeply dependent upon each other. Just as violence and sectarianism are contagious, so peace is also contagious. Peaceful human relationships make complex negotiations effective and common-sense solutions possible. Leaders frequently cannot move as far or as fast as we would like them to, they need the help of the rest of us to free up new possibilities. The peace process will succeed, as long as our spirit and determination remains unbroken. Thank you.

Jim Gibney

The first point I would like to make is that when I first received the invitation to speak tonight I thought I would be doing so against a background of absolute political despair, with the institutions collapsed due to David Trimble's actions and all of us in a dangerous political vacuum. I am glad to said that the IRA initiative a week ago on Tuesday saved the day, saved the peace process, gave everyone who supports the Good Friday Agreement an opportunity to re-dedicate themselves to working all the institutions for all the people of this island, Nationalist and Unionist, Republican and Loyalist. Now, you might say that such a judgement is too premature because we have yet to get through tomorrow's vote at the Assembly. But the important difference is that if David Trimble doesn't get elected because of internal opposition, Republicans will have a quite different view of that outcome than if David Trimble and his party had brought the institutions down. There are different messages coming out of the two sets of circumstances. It is difficult to predict tomorrow's result, but it will be an appalling act of irresponsibility if Unionists elected on a 'yes' ticket refuse to back their leader. By their actions they would be sending entirely the wrong message – that politics and negotiations don't work. And we all know there are people waiting in the wings to drag us back into a violent situation.

A live peace process, with all the complications associated with it, is preferable to one that is in freefall. Tonight's theme – 'Whatever happened to the peace process?' – can be viewed in two ways: positively or negatively. And it would be easy to list all the things that are wrong with the peace process, but I don't intend to do that tonight. I want to highlight a few of the positive things I think have happened over the last number of years. I believe that not enough focus has been put on the achievements of the peace process to date. Now, obviously, I am making my remarks against the background of the UDA's bombing campaign against the Catholic and Nationalist people of the Six Counties, their siege of Nationalists in North Belfast, and their blockading of the Holy Cross school children. That is the context within which we meet tonight.

I believe there are more pluses than minuses for the peace process. The difficulties we are experiencing on the ground, and, indeed, within the political system itself, can, and will be, resolved. And the framework and the dynamic that will be used to resolve them lie at the heart of the peace process itself. For me, and I have been a Republican activist since I was sixteen, the greatest benefit by far is that fewer people are being killed or injured, or going to prison as a result of political conflict here. Now, that is no small achievement, even in the circumstances I outlined at the start.

The greatest benefit [of the peace process] by far is that fewer people are being killed or injured, or going to prison as a result of political conflict here.

And I know it is always dodgy to make comparisons between one country and another, but there is supposedly a peace process in Palestine/Israel yet people die there every day of the week. And in South Africa during their peace process thousands of people, mainly black, were killed. Indeed, there were more blacks killed in the years *after* Nelson Mandela was released than there were during the entire period of apartheid. Now, of course, there are explanations as to why these killings happened, and are still happening in Palestine/Israel, but the point I am making is that those people, particularly those who Republicans have described as 'securocrats' here in this country, are unable to create the circumstances which would drag us all into a violent vortex. I believe that they are trying to create these circumstances and some Loyalists are helping them, but the strength of the peace process is preventing them from being successful.

Another important development arising from the peace process is that we can all genuinely set our hands and minds to establishing a meaningful process of national reconciliation on this island between the two great political and cultural traditions, and that can only be achieved in the circumstances where a peace process is in place and political institutions are shaped to facilitate this objective. In my opinion, these institutions have been identified, although they are not yet fully functioning. From a Republican perspective we believe that the most important institution is the all-Ireland ministerial council, because it is through this institution that the objective that we seek as Republicans – a United Ireland – can be worked for, peacefully and energetically.

In addition to this institution, there is the Executive and the Assembly. During the negotiations which led up to the Good Friday Agreement Sinn Féin negotiators vigorously opposed the idea of an Executive and an Assembly. We did so on the basis that we believed both institutions would be turned into sectarian bearpits and that progress would be delayed. However, we now believe, even with the limited amount of time both institutions have been in place, that the Executive and the Assembly are not only important, but indispensable, and an essential part of the political and human jigsaw. We did not believe this during the negotiations but we believe it now and we are committed to these institutions, and no-one should underestimate how difficult it has been for Republicans to make the decisions they have made over the last number of years. Ten years ago the words 'peace' and 'compromise' were not part of the Republican dictionary; they are today.

We believe that the Executive and the Assembly are... an essential part of the political and human jigsaw. We did not believe this during the negotiations but we believe it now and we are committed to these institutions, and no-one should underestimate how difficult it has been for Republicans to make the decisions they have made over the last number of years.

There is another important development arising from the peace process. Politics is in the first place about people, it is not some abstract theory to be taken off the shelf and occasionally debated. Politicians, and not just those who get elected, but the people in this room and elsewhere, have a moral obligation to change society so that people's everyday lives are changed for the better. That, I believe, is what has happened, and is happening to the peace process, and that the people who live in the community have a better quality of life as a result. Go Raibh Agat.

Brian Feeney

I want to look at some of the things that have happened to the peace process since 1998, since the Agreement was signed, and also to say that the peace process isn't simply a unit. It's divided in two: there is a peace process and there is a political process. And the political process goes in little jumps and then stops for a while, and then jumps forward again. The political process can actually stall, but the peace process goes on.

Now, I had always thought when the Agreement was signed and the Referendum was held that it would take about five years for the whole thing to bed down. I now realise it is going to take much longer. So, what has happened, why is it extended? I blame the British. One of the recurring views I have is that if the British government had put a fraction of the energy into driving the peace process *since* 1998 that they had put into establishing the peace process *before* 1998 we wouldn't be where we are now. They put their best people in, they brought over extra civil servants, they worked enormously hard between June 1997 and the Spring of 1998, to get an Agreement through and passed.

Since then, disgracefully, we've had three Secretaries of State, we've had umpteen civil servants, at the top, and not one of them has got any reason for the whole thing to succeed. It is something that someone else has done. Before 1998 there was complete agreement between the two governments that there had to be this Agreement, that this was the moment that had to be seized. But after 1998 you had people operating for their own political reasons, sometimes fooling about with bits of the Agreement, and allowing the whole thing to extend. Now, there are a number of issues in the Agreement which were fairly fraught, like policing, or criminal justice, human rights and so on. Once the Agreement was signed the British government allowed those elements to drift, they didn't drive them. The effect of that was that the Unionist population saw each of these as a 'sop to Republicans' and tried to dismantle these elements. Because they were partially successful under someone like Mandelson in stalling some of those elements a lot of people on the Loyalist side and some people within mainstream Unionism said that Britishness and Unionism was being salami-sliced, being taken away bit by bit over the last three years. And what I would contend is that if the Agreement had been properly driven, things would have been different. For one, the reformed Criminal Justice process is still not in force. The new Police Service is only coming into operation, partially, tomorrow. There are other aspects that are still not through.

> ***If the British government had put a fraction of the energy into driving the peace process* since *1998 that they had put into establishing the peace process* before *1998 we wouldn't be where we are now.***

Once they got the Agreement, and it was an amazing achievement, what you do is to start to build buttresses around it, you start to make sure the brickwork isn't going to collapse, you build on it. And, in fact, the opposite happened, it was allowed to drift. Partly that was the fault of the British government but it's also the fault of the political parties here. One of the things which constantly surprised me, particularly on the Nationalist side, and especially with Republicans, is that they didn't demand a root and branch reform of the Northern Ireland Office. One of the main problems here is that the place is run by English civil servants. There is one particular character who was involved in advising Humphrey Atkins during the Hunger Strike some twenty years ago – and he's still here. I don't know if any of you remember reading the famous document which was leaked in 1997, concerning Garvaghy Road, the 'scenario document', about 'putting Orange feet' on the Garvaghy Road. It was written by this same civil servant who has been making a mess of things for twenty years. Now, these guys just have to be taken away. There isn't a single Nationalist in the Northern Ireland Office, there isn't a single Northern Ireland person in the top echelons... There is actually an amazing security category which is called 'UK Eyes Only' which doesn't include people from Northern Ireland, much to the fury of Northern Ireland civil servants.

Civil servants have been allowed to be in charge of it, not local civil servants but English civil servants based in Great George's Street, London, who don't know what this place is like.

So, there are a number of things which have happened to the process. It has been allowed to drift, it is not being driven by the British government. Civil servants have been allowed to be in charge of it, not local civil servants but English civil servants based in Great George's Street, London, who don't know what this place is like. But the effect of that has been very bad on Unionists, for two reasons. First, it has pulled apart what was a unit in the Agreement, and left Unionists thinking: right, we can actually change parts of this Agreement, we can stall, we can veto parts of this Agreement – and they have been allowed to do that in some cases, and make major alterations. Secondly, large number of Unionists have thought: wait a minute, as we see this Agreement slowly coming into operation we're the losers here, everything seems to be going the one way, everything is being taken away from us and being handed, slowly but surely, over to Nationalists.

My contention is that if there had been – if you'll pardon the expression – a 'big bang' in 1998/99 and the whole thing came into operation, this salami-slicing stuff wouldn't have happened, and you wouldn't have been able to say: oh, it's all drifting away from Unionists and Nationalists are getting everything, because the whole thing would have come into operation as it was intended, and everyone would have benefited.

Now, there's another aspect of what has gone wrong with the Agreement, and that is the fundamental failure within mainstream Unionism to educate their own supporters. There is a contradiction between what David Trimble and some

Unionists are doing, and what they're saying. I mean, they are actually working the Agreement in most respects, but they still haven't even shaken hands with the senior Sinn Féin figures who they're sitting round the table with in the Executive. So, the example that they are providing to the other Unionists outside is: look, we're having to do this, we have to sit down with these people, but we really don't want anything to do with them. And in many ways that justifies the opposition of extreme Loyalists, who say: well, at least we're honest, we don't want anything to do with it, whereas David Trimble pretends he's involved, and pretends he's not involved at the same time. So there's an inherent contradiction in the position that Trimble has taken up – he's in the Executive but he's not off the Executive.

Now, what he has to do, and what Unionism has to do, is work really hard to educate their electorate, the sort of thing Republicans were doing from the early 90s. Republicans took a long time to educate people, to eventually turn them around. Nobody's doing that on the Unionist side, and you really need to have senior figures like David Trimble coming out and saying: look, we have to live on equal terms with these people; we're equal to them, they're equal to us; we're nothing more, we're nothing less. And that's what we have to do instead of trying to say: well, we're really worried about some of the people these Nationalists elect, we'd like them to elect somebody else, we don't actually want to shake hands with Sinn Féin, we just have to put up with them. Until mainstream Unionism comes out and leads its people, its voters, into saying that we don't want anything else other than to be equal to these people, we're not going to get anywhere. At the moment it isn't doing that. Until the Spring of this year there was a narrow majority of Unionists in favour, but by the summer there is a clear, overwhelming majority of Unionists against the Agreement. Why is that? It's not because there's been violence, it's not because Republicans have welshed on the deal. It's because nobody on the Unionist side is sitting down and saying: right, this is what has to happen, and educating people. And, I repeat again, the fundamental thing is that we don't want to be anything more than equal to anybody else on this island.

Until mainstream Unionism comes out and leads its people into saying that we don't want anything else other than to be equal to these people, we're not going to get anywhere.

Pete Shirlow

I think I am going to be slightly more cynical. I think there is a lot of illusion surrounding the peace process. I am very happy there *is* a peace process and I'm very happy that there's obviously significant changes, but, as an illustration, last week a friend of mine rang me up – he was an ex-IRA prisoner who worked on a project – and he asked: do you think the IRA is going to decommission? And I thought to myself: well, if *you* don't know, I don't know. Half an hour later I got a phone call from a friend who is a Unionist, and he said: do you think if the IRA decommission the Unionist Party will go back to the Executive? And you're thinking that these people are much closer to the thing and yet they don't know any more than I know. And that's one of the things I ask about the peace process: just *who* is making the decisions about what's actually happening?

Another thing which concerns me is that the peace process might actually deradicalise our society. I am interested in left-wing politics, and I feel disappointed when I see each party being supportive of PFI*, or when I see their approach to the budget. I think questions have to be asked, such as: how are we going to deliver better services to people, how are we going to create equality in this society, not just in terms of religion, but in terms of gender and social class.

I think that what we have now are ideologies of equal strength; Republicans now have an ideology which is of equal strength politically in relation to votes as it is for Unionists and Loyalists. So politically, as well as in terms of demography, we can no longer have a Unionist dominance over society.

If you look at the political process, the Belfast Agreement, we see immediate problems. Those who support the Belfast Agreement on the Unionist/Loyalist side do so because they see devolution as protecting Unionism, they see that this Agreement upholds the majority's desire to remain within the UK. Whereas Nationalists and Republicans see in the power-sharing Executive something which is going to be a medium-term institution which, coupled with population change, is going to eventually carry them into a United Ireland. Or take the border issue. For Unionists, by getting rid of Articles 2 and 3, the border is confirmed. But Republicans and Nationalists see the Ministerial Council as giving an Irish dimension to northern affairs. Hence, the border as an issue still exists. So, the people who support the peace process are supporting it for different reasons. Obviously, some support it for humanitarian reasons and a desire to get beyond conflict and create a post-conflict society, but when people actually see what it means constitutionally it is still problematic.

Questions have to be asked, such as: how are we going to deliver better services to people, how are we going to create equality in this society, not just in terms of religion, but in terms of gender and social class.

I think the Agreement is really a treaty between the UK and the Irish Republic. On the one hand we have an endorsement of Irish national determination, and on the other we have an endorsement of the British Constitutional Convention; two things which are completely different but are now endorsed within our constitutional change. Unionists sees themselves as being protected by the

* Private Finance Initiative, under which services formally provided by public service workers are being tendered out to the private sector.

principle of consent, in that they are currently the majority. But the principle of consent can equally work to the advantage of those who *become* the majority.

The Agreement is also positive because it creates a federal relationship that places us further away from Westminster, that gives us some form of localisation of our politics, that gives us some local control over what we do. But at the same time it doesn't necessarily make it clear what is going to happen in terms of atavism, in terms of political groups being different to each other.

I actually think the peace process is about management – the British and Irish states have come up with what they think is the best solution to manage this society. And what we have at the moment is basically a holding operation, and we have a situation where we have something which is not going to last, because we all know there is going to be constitutional change at some time in the future. And the way the future of this society is going to be determined is through plebiscite politics, or border polls, or referendums. So there's an inherent instability there for the future.

So I think that we have many things which are positive, and many things that are negative. And we still don't have an agreement about what the last thirty years was all about, it is still a very subjective understanding. Who were the good guys, who were the bad guys? That still hasn't been resolved, there's no level of conflict resolution going on to bring people to feel able to say: the other community are victims in the same way that my community is a victim. Indeed, I think the politics of this society have shifted into new forms of the old conflict. It is now a conflict over Orange marches, over little girls going to school, a conflict over access to jobs, All of those things have been there before in the background, but they are the things that are always going to re-emerge.

I actually think the peace process is about management – the British and Irish states have come up with what they think is the best solution to manage this society. And what we have at the moment is basically a holding operation.

One difficult question I see for Republicans is that, having created a resistance culture, how do you deconstruct that? Ten, fifteen years on their own constituency is going to be saying: where are these new hospitals, these new jobs, this better society that I was promised? And the Brits are still here. I'm not saying that that's going to drive people into the arms of dissidents but I think these are very important questions that are going to have to be looked at, for this is where conflict is going to be. We can see that already – it's back to the 1960s, access over housing, jobs, that's the sort of politics we seem to be going back to.

I think we need to consider some other issues. Where is the equality agenda in this? We thought we would get a minister who would look into equality, but we didn't – the equality issue went into the office of the First Minister. Yet equality is a major issue which divides this society.

Nor does the peace process address problems of communal rights; we have issues of political culture which have been unanswered. We have a peace process which doesn't really solve the problem of territorial society. We have a Minister of State who a few weeks ago called people who were rioting at the peaceline 'scum'. Now, we can all criticise that violence, but these people are a product of what happened in this society over the last thirty years. Has the British state not been involved? Where has the British state gone to, in the whole analysis of the conflict? Did they not help create the current situation? They seem to have disappeared out of the equation. And I think both states have tried to make this more of a 'native' problem: it's those Northern Irish, they're at it again. And I think we need to reinvestigate that. The state has done things in the past which were wrong, so why are *they* not being questioned in terms of what's actually happening now?

Most of all, I think what we have is that the people who suffered most in this conflict are the people who are continuing to suffer. There was a survey done by my university recently. It revealed that 70% of the people who died in this city lived within 500 metres of a peaceline; that the places where the conflict largely took place are places where unemployment levels are three times higher than the average for this city. And it still impacts today: 60% of the people who live in a peaceline area won't shop, or won't visit, the community on the other side. I have never heard any Secretary of State or any government minister talk about this. Workplaces that are available in Catholic areas have an average Protestant workforce of less than 10%. Workplaces that are available in Protestant areas have a workforce of Catholics of less than 6%. So we are constantly being told that the peace process is going to bring us jobs, bring us prosperity, stability, but nobody is moving across the peacelines. If you look at equality legislation nowhere is it mentioned about chill factors, nowhere is it mentioned that sectarianism and fear influences the way people live in this society. So, like everything else, the realities in this society are somewhere else.

70% of the people who died in this city lived within 500 metres of a peaceline; the places where the conflict largely took place are places where unemployment levels are three times higher than the average for this city.

And I think that the reasons we haven't come to terms with those issues, is because these are the difficult issues, these are the issues which could rip this society apart again. So, I suppose, for the state there is a question of trying to push things under the carpet.

I suppose what we finally have to come back to is the issue of victimhood. I think there is obviously a great deal of sorrow and bitterness in this society and the time when I will put my hand up and say 'yes, this thing is working', is when you hear people getting up and saying that: yes, their community has been perpetrators as well as victims, because I think in this society you can be both.

So we have to move beyond something which is merely managed, towards something which tries to create a society in which people can live normal lives, they can move to places, they can go to places, and have and enjoy the experience of living in a new society. And I think we're a long way from that and when we get there then I think we'll be living in a society in which there has been a peace process. Thank you.

Beverely Milton-Edwards

I am not going to talk directly about our peace process here, but indirectly, by reflecting on the positives and the negatives in another peace process – that involving Palestinians and Israelis, which is the context in which I have an expertise and have been involved in for the last fifteen years.

I want to start off with an anecdote about a small group of Palestinians and Israelis who came to Belfast for five days in the summer of 1999. This group came in secret to Belfast and negotiations were held here as part of the 'second tract' diplomacy on the future of Jerusalem. The people who were involved in this negotiating process, some of whom were themselves the architects of the Oslo Process, and some of whom were high-ranking figures on the Palestinian side, spent the first three days of their visit here touring the city, visiting the police, City Hall, the Housing Executive, community projects, visiting the Ardoyne, Tigers Bay, LEDU – looking at all the dimensions of life in the city. And at the end of those three days we had a session where we got them to reflect on their feelings about the place, and I was really surprised to hear them all agree – indeed, there was a major consensus on both sides – that whatever happened in the final stages of the negotiations on Jerusalem, that they never wanted to experience the polarisation and the atavistic hatred they felt they had seen in Belfast.

They said that: we never want Jerusalem to be as bad as Belfast. Despite the prosperity of the city they were shocked by the peacelines, they were shocked by the fact that there were these deliberately constructed barriers separating people.

I was absolutely stunned to hear these people depicting a society that I have lived in now for ten years in that way, I just couldn't believe it. And this was one of the focus points they took away with them, they said that: we never want Jerusalem to be as bad as Belfast. Despite the prosperity of the city they were shocked by the peacelines, they were shocked by the fact that there were these deliberately constructed barriers separating people. They were shocked at how militarised our city appeared to them, despite the prosperity, despite the urban regeneration, the nightclubs, the bars, the cafés, the revitalised centre of our city, the hotels. They just couldn't handle it.

Now the somewhat disappointing aspect of that anecdote is that in April of this year I met with those same people again in London. This was a very difficult meeting, it was very difficult to get people to come, the second intifada by that point had been ongoing for about six months. And, of course, Belfast and the peace process came up in the discussions and the debate. And opinions had started changing about Belfast and how bad it was, and they now felt that *at least there had been a process here* within which more than a few elements of society had been involved in determining the negotiation, the dialogue, the process to try and end conflict.

And what I am trying to say here is that we need to acknowledge that 'process' – the notion of process in achieving or negotiating a political solution to conflict – is not just important but essential. And however we define that process we have to have it, there has to be a set of frameworks that are commonly agreed, negotiated and discussed. Because at the moment what's happening in the West Bank and Gaza and in Israel is that there is no process. And people are lost, they are genuinely lost, they are stuck in an impasse of violence and they just don't know how to get out of it. And the kind of violence that is taking place at the moment is unbelievable. We're talking about helicopter gunships, suicide bombings, rocket attacks, F16 warplanes. People on both sides are completely lost and they want a process back.

And opinions had started changing about Belfast and how bad it was, and they now felt that* at least there had been a process here *within which more than a few elements of society had been involved in determining the negotiation, the dialogue, the process to try and end conflict.

There is a recognition now that it is not necessarily the *nature* of the process which is the problem, but the *agenda* that it is designed to facilitate; a recognition that the Oslo agenda, in fact, has *not* been about inclusiveness, about representation of all elements of society, or about an anticipated outcome of democratic governance. What people have begun to realise, finally, is that this was never what the Oslo agenda was about, it was about meeting somebody else's national interests and concerns, it wasn't about conflict resolution, it wasn't about finding and creating and building trust and reaching resolution on the issues which brought the Israelis and Palestinians into conflict in the first place. There's no positive spin which can be put on the Oslo process.

We've heard discussion here about the negatives and the positives, but there is at least an acknowledgment that there have been improvements in this society – politically, economically, legislatively, in terms of international support. But there have been no improvements on either side for the Israelis or the Palestinians, there's no dividend to this process. In which case I would question whether we can really meaningfully call what exists there a 'peace process', when both sides seem to be losing, losing in terms of human life, economically, politically... drifting, feeling abandoned and bereft of support.

And that brings me to another point about the role of external actors and this has been an issue that has been raised this evening in the context of the role of the British government and the Irish government. And I would say that compared to the Palestinian/Israeli process at least we've had the benefit of balanced intervention, both sides in some way have enjoyed or have been able to call upon external mediation, facilitation, at points where it has been difficult for us to do it ourselves. That's not the case in the Israeli/Palestinian context. There is no balanced intervention, and this is hampering attempts to move out of the impasse, it is hampering attempts to find genuine routes out of their conflict. Because those who are intervening are not genuine about the outcome, they are, to use Pete's phrase, simply trying to 'manage' the conflict.

[The] Oslo agenda was about meeting somebody else's national interests and concerns, it wasn't about creating and building trust and reaching resolution on the issues which brought the Israelis and Palestinians into conflict in the first place.

The United States, particularly before September 11th, was in fact abrogating its democratic responsibility to drive this process forward, it was unofficially understood that the Americans were quite happy to stand back and let this loss of life continue. I'm not talking about a handful of casualties or fatalities here, I'm talking about the loss of hundreds of Palestinian and Israeli lives. And in a sense it is not just the Americans who abrogated their responsibilities, it is the entire international community, including the United Nations. In fact for as long as we continue to abrogate this responsibility the crisis that currently besets the Middle East will continue. The conflict will remain caught in this reactive spiral of violence. Because again the leadership in both communities is just not up to the task. The leadership is completely out of touch on the Palestinian side with its own constituency, it is bankrupt, it is corrupt, there is a crisis of confidence on the streets, and popularly it is believed that Arafat has lost control. On the Israeli side Ariel Sharon is living in the past, and it is generally acknowledged that he's not interested in the future, that he's quite happy to take Israel back to the 1970s and 1980s. He talks of his so-called 'partners in peace' as nothing more than animals, and has declared his 'partner for peace', Arafat, a terrorist.

So the vocabulary of peace is missing in terms of leadership, the support that is needed from the international community is absent, and yet we throw our hands up in despair when we watch our TV and we blame these people for this violence. There's no process because we're not willing to support it or facilitate it. And as long as we don't do that we can't expect them to solve it themselves. And I think that's where I would like to leave it.

* * * * * * * *

Barbara McCabe Any questions for the panel?

Male Not so much a question as an observation. People like myself who work on the ground, who do cross-community work, who try to rebuild and regenerate our communities, have a terrible feeling of frustration about everything that is happening at the moment. The feeling that I get on the ground is that people aren't really worried about Ian Paisley, they're worried about the Ulster Unionist Party, who are not trying to implement the Agreement. To my mind, it appears the strategy between them and Paisley is only a difference of style, they don't want the Agreement to work, they don't want Catholics about the place, they don't want equality. So that's a very real fear. My other concern is the total absence of any reference by both governments to conflict resolution on the scale it would need to be tackled. No normal society would have any time for all the nonsense that is going on in Ardoyne or anywhere else. But unless we develop a whole strategy towards countering that – through schools, through parents, through communities – then this society is not going to move on. So there's a real frustration among people like myself who work on the ground.

My other concern is the total absence of any reference by both governments to conflict resolution on the scale it would need to be tackled.

Roy Garland As a member of the Unionist Party I don't think it is true to say that the Ulster Unionist Party leadership, the pro-Agreement element, doesn't want it to work, and 'doesn't want a Taig about the place', I don't think that's true at all. But the Unionist Party is deeply divided. For example, my branch is overwhelmingly anti-Agreement, with hard-liners taking over lock, stock and barrel. At one stage I had a bit of freedom to do things, but not now. If David Trimble had done more of the things I think he should have done, I'm not sure he wouldn't have been where I am – more isolated within the Unionist Party. He managed to stay in there. Nevertheless, I believe there is a genuine desire to make the thing work, and things *have* changed enormously. In 1996 I proposed at the Unionist Council – with hundreds of people there – that we talk to Sinn Féin. There was near uproar, everybody opposed what I had said. But things are changing, although perhaps not quick enough and things on the outside are going to pieces here and there. But where we are now compared to where we were then is enormously different. Trimble hasn't shaken hands with Sinn Féin, which I think is incredible, but he has talked with them, he meets Gerry Adams privately – that is an amazing thing, coming from where they were before.

Jim Gibney I would agree with what Roy is saying in terms of substantial sections of Unionist opinion being prepared to work the Agreement, being prepared to support the peace process. I think there is clear evidence of that, not least of which the fact that the Executive was in place for a period of time, not least the fact that among quite a number of the Ulster Unionist Party MLAs there is a working relationship on the various committees at the Executive. And Sinn Féin and Nationalists are there working with them. And for that matter the DUP, I have to say, also work the system, and don't, certainly on the inside, try to wreck it. But where I have a problem is with the quality of leadership that David Trimble brings to bear on that section of positive Unionism and Loyalism. I think that he kept looking over his shoulder... and the way in which he handled the question of the IRA's arms fed the 'no' element within both the Unionism people and organised political Unionism, and that more than anything else has led us to this impasse. But tomorrow, of course, is a big day in terms of the peace process. With the issue of IRA arms at long last put where it should have been put all along – with de Chastelain – the test now is whether or not that section of 'yes' Unionism is prepared to do what Brian Feeney referred to, which is treat the rest of the people of this island, particularly those in the North, as equal citizens.

With the issue of IRA arms at long last put where it should have been put all along... the test now is whether or not 'yes' Unionism is prepared to treat the rest of the people of this island, particularly those in the North, as equal citizens.

Pete Shirlow Of course, when you go into the Protestant community they will tell you that it is Sinn Féin who don't want the peace process to work; the argument that you are making has a mirror argument within Unionism, that this thing is being stalled by the other side. And that's how they see it, so there's more to this than not wanting to push the thing forward, there's other complexities. People have talked over and over again about confidence. I actually think Sinn Féin got much less out of the Agreement than the Unionists, but they can sell something much more effectively than Unionists. One of the things I notice increasingly when teaching in University is that young middle-class Protestants who would be from Unionist families, aren't interested in politics, do not have any sense of being Unionist, do not have any sense of responsibility to get involved in politics, don't care if there's a United Ireland, don't care if they're in the UK. They live in a consumerist world, a world which is MTV, drinking in The Fly... This is where they're at, yet when you get the same people from a Nationalist background they're more likely to talk about politics, about their community moving forward. There's a negatively within Protestantism which assumes 'these people' will take over one day.

Male Roy and Jim were very optimistic but I could take you now to North Belfast and there is no optimism there for the peace process. You can't move forward in society when things are still happening such as in North Belfast on a daily basis. We're talking about a situation which is worse than I have ever seen it before. We're talking about 90 pipe-bomb attacks, and what's happening at higher political levels is of no consequence to North Belfast. So my question is: how do you get that sense of optimism back into the communities? It's not there. People involved in community work feel very depressed, we don't see where we're going, and the fact that some deal was done last week don't change the situation on the ground.

Male I have listened to the panel and I talk to people in North Belfast on a daily basis and I never hear them talking about this moving forward. The biggest concern in North Belfast at the moment is to protect your home, that's the biggest thing in people's minds. The politicians aren't living in the areas where it's happening, they really don't know what is going on. It's a serious situation there. The other thing I didn't like was when the speakers talked about South Africa – that there was more people killed after Mandela got released – as if this is what happens in these peace processes and we have to accept it. I don't think we have to accept any of it at all.

In societies which have been locked into armed conflict for many years but which are now trying to move into a peaceful environment... there will always be vested interests who will attempt to slow that process down

Jim Gibney It was me who made the reference to South Africa and the situation in Palestine/Israel. I made those points to illustrate that in societies which have been locked into armed conflict for many years but which are now trying to move into a peaceful environment wherein normal politics can take shape there will always be vested interests who will attempt to slow that process down. There are vested interests who will ensure that there are people killed, intimidated, whatever, they will create a violent situation in which the change that is heralded – in our situation, by the Good Friday Agreement – is delayed on the ground. So what you have in North Belfast, although not with the same level of deaths, is similar to what happened in the Natal province of South Africa, where thousands of people were killed. The people in the security establishment there who didn't want to see the kind of changes which came to South Africa with black majority rule, are the same type of people who are using the Loyalists in North Belfast to create that siege situation there on the ground, the exact same people. The purpose behind it was to get the result that they got in terms of the policing issue, because Patten said we need this type of a police force, but the elements in the NIO that Brian was talking about didn't want to see Patten implemented. So how do you slow down or prevent Patten from being implemented? You create a violent situation that makes people say: oh, you can't do that, look at the violence there. There is a reason behind this violence, there is a purpose behind it. The second point that I would make with regard to North Belfast is that strenuous efforts are being made, with Sinn Féin and the SDLP on the Nationalist side, while Billy Hutchinson and others, including some clergy, are doing their best on the Loyalist side. And, in fact, there was a deal there three weeks ago to have the problem sorted out at Holy Cross, with a view to trying to get some sort of forum for people to meet. That deal was scuppered by elements of the UDA because it didn't suit them. So, it's not as if people are not trying, they are trying their best, and I know there is a fear factor in the North Belfast, you can taste it. But we don't have total control there, there are people there with a different political purpose.

Beverely Milton-Edwards What we have seen since 1998 is that a distance has been growing between the community and our political representatives whose work or objectives or agendas have been solely focused on keeping the 'process' going, and have become increasingly neglectful of the communities that they are supposed to represent. Now that is something which is extremely common. It happened in South Africa, it certainly happened during the Oslo process within the West Bank and Gaza Strip, where a once-vibrant community sector on the Palestinian side, and actually on the Israeli side – the community sector, the non-governmental sector which actually was the deliverer of the peace agreement – found itself increasingly marginalised by the political leadership, and by donor communities and agents. And, to some extent we have seen that here as well. We have seen, as Pete was saying earlier on, those who lost most lose more still, and that's exactly the same. We have to be careful with the peace process. We seem to be saying that as long as there are no problems with the [political] process then we can move forward, we can address issues, but the minute there are problems with that process we have to stop and wait and see what happens, that we can't move unilaterally. And I have heard people saying that here in the community, and I would question that approach. We need to urge our representatives to support those people who are trying to resolve these issues [at the grassroots], because that's what we are always going to be coming back to, *irrespective* of the [political] process.

A distance has been growing between the community and our political representatives whose work or objectives or agendas have been solely focused on keeping the 'process' going, and have become increasingly neglectful of the communities that they are supposed to represent.

Brian Feeney North Belfast is absolutely disgraceful. It is entirely the responsibility of the British administration here, for they are responsible for security here. It is nothing to do with local representatives. And the security people know *exactly* what is happening in North Belfast. They know the names of the UDA men who are organising it, and all through the summer they did nothing. And they dithered about specifying the UDA... there was this joke that the UDA were on ceasefire through the summer despite scores and scores of pipe-bombs being thrown. They've done nothing about that – has anybody been convicted of throwing a pipe-bomb this year? This was allowed to escalate throughout the whole summer, so you had some of the worst rioting in North Belfast since 1986. And why did 1986 see bad rioting? Because it was after the Anglo-Irish Agreement of 1985, and throughout 1986 and into July 1986 the worst rioting was in Manor Street in almost exactly the same situation. But local representatives have no control over security. You can go and beat your brains out with the Security Minister Jane Kennedy, or the Secretary of State John Reid, but all to no avail. It all comes down to their failure to deal with Loyalist violence; they don't know how to do it, and they have never known how to do it.

Beverely Milton-Edwards Brian, can I ask you then are you saying that the situation in North Belfast is *just* a security issue, because I don't see it as that. There are education issues, employment issues, as well...

Brian Feeney I'll tell you what could be done immediately. There is a row of houses behind Newington that should be demolished tomorrow, there's nobody in them, they are being used to throw pipe-bombs into the Nationalist area. There's a Catholic enclave on the other side of the Limestone Road which could be totally protected. There's a street leading out of Tigers Bay onto the Limestone Road and there should have been a wall built across it; there should have been a wall built across it fifteen years ago. Now, you will not be able to deal with education or employment *until* you resolve that problem. Only when you've got that done can you start talking about education and community development.

You will not be able to deal with education or employment until you resolve [the] problem [of security]. Only when you've got that done can you start talking about education and community development.

Roy Garland What you're saying, Brian, is that without security you can't deal with other issues?

Beverely Milton-Edwards That's what the Israelis and the Palestinians are saying at the moment, and it's not getting anybody anywhere.

Female I am American and a lot of Americans who have been following what is going on at Holy Cross ask the simple question: why are the police not arresting these people? I find it hard to understand why, if you want to get to the other issues such as education, housing, and whatever, people don't seem to accept that you first need to go in and arrest the people who are causing the problems, they are breaking the law. And it's a very odd situation to witness, especially when everybody is talking about peace and trying to get a new government in place, and a new system of law, and yet nobody is enforcing this law, it is as if they are afraid to enforce it. I would say there is a lawless society in areas like North Belfast. I know there's far more too it, but...

Jim Gibney I want to respond to this North Belfast situation again because a point that has been made by a number of people who have spoken is that it is being orchestrated. There are of course problems there, but there are problems all over the city. But the problems that people are experiencing in South, East and West Belfast, people are talking to each other and trying to sort them out. So, clearly, there is a group of people in the North of the city who think that what they're doing is advantageous to their position. But they have free will. They can back the deal put three weeks' ago, because it is in everyone's interest that that is implemented in full. And I just think that you can't walk away from reality and the point I was making about other people having an agenda – at a Northern Ireland Office level if you like, the military people... It was no accident that a certain person in the NIO, who was the main military person on the ground in this country for the last ten or fifteen years, was the first person who met the Sinn Féin delegation, and it was no accident that he more than anyone else blocked the negotiations. These are the people who are in place, this has been a military situation for hundreds of years, but particularly this last thirty. So, these guys are in there and they're working to an agenda and if politicians and community leaders step back from that reality then they are deluding themselves. North Belfast can be solved in the morning; it requires a change in attitude by the UDA on the ground. Once they change their attitude then that situation will, in my understanding of it anyway, be speedily quietened down.

These guys are in there and they're working to an agenda and if politicians and community leaders step back from that reality then they are deluding themselves.

Male I am suspicious of this talk about a securocrat agenda, and I'm a bit suspicious about putting what's happening in North Belfast down to a handful of hoods. Now, I don't know about a securocrat agenda and I don't know what goes on in MI5 or the NIO or wherever, and I think it is acknowledged that the UDA is playing a leading and nefarious role in whipping up what is going on in North Belfast. But for years when I was growing up people used to tell me: oh, see the thing with the IRA, there's only just a handful of them, you know, they don't really have that much support, it's only a few rotten eggs in the basket that's stirring up all this trouble – it's a criminalisation thing. And I am sitting here listening to similar arguments being talked about the situation in the Loyalist community. Yes, there may be things going on – the role of paramilitaries, the role of hoods, whatever – but at the end of the day there are *real* fears, and *real* insecurities, and *real* angers within the Protestant community within North Belfast, that at the end of the day Republican negotiators, their representatives and people like me who live in comfortable areas around town are going to have to engage with. And I think if we get too much locked into the 'hood' and 'securocrat agenda' type of talk, it means we don't have to engage with it, it means we can sideline it, it means we can say; to be honest, at the end of the day it doesn't really exist, this is another sort of problem. So I think there is a trap there and we need to be careful about not falling into it.

I think if we get too much locked into the 'hood' and 'securocrat agenda' type of talk, it means we don't have to engage with it, it means we can sideline it, it means we can say; to be honest, at the end of the day it doesn't really exist, this is another sort of problem. So I think there is a trap there and we need to be careful about not falling into it.

Roy Garland I suppose that many Unionists identify with the British establishment, and I don't think that all Unionists would accept some of the things that are being said here about the securocrats, I don't think they believe that, there would be a lot of scepticism.

Brian Feeney I don't think people believe that there's only a couple of people in the UDA walking through North Belfast, and anybody who watched the last parade through Tiger Bay of hundreds of UDA men in full uniform, it's obviously not three guys running about from street to street. It is always quite interesting to watch a parade like that, it's unimaginable to imagine 600 members of the IRA marching down the Falls Road, but Loyalists are allowed to do it. They can do it in Tiger Bay, they can do it on the Shankill Road, thousands of them. But I think what should have been done and it's part of the Agreement that hasn't worked, and this was a commitment in the Agreement to integrate former prisoners back into society. Now, because that wasn't done, the UDA, for whom there is nothing in the Agreement – they didn't get anybody elected, their big efforts to go political went nowhere, they didn't make it – so there is nothing in it for them. But if the government had genuinely made an effort to reintegrate former prisoners into society, by which I mean providing things for them to do, providing cash, there might have been more people in the UDA prepared to think the Agreement works, rather than get into drug dealing. And to involve themselves genuinely in community work than what they do now, because there's nothing in it. These guys were vital to the process before the ceasefires in 1994, they are vital now and they are simply being neglected by the government. And every time there is an attempt to put some money into activities or groups or whatever involving former prisoners there's uproar, and everybody says: what about the victims, there should be millions given to victims? The fact is that former prisoners are victims as well.

Male I think the kind of question that needs to be asked is what brings a community to the level that it feels it has to stop kids from going to school, and what brings parents to the level that they feel they have to insist on bringing their kids through that situation? Let's look at the problem, and start dealing with that problem. I have no doubt that there is some kind of secret hand behind this. I watched on the Deerpark Road, there were attacks every other night, you could have an undercover group sitting there picking them up, just by anticipating it happening, but they're getting away with it that much because it's obvious they've been told there's going to be a clear run for them. So there is a securocrat agenda there, I have no doubt about that. I'm not sure what that agenda is though, because I suspect that it is an agenda to destroy Loyalism and Unionism. And I speak as a Loyalist, I resent what is being done in the name of Loyalism, it is misrepresenting Loyalism. I think also in terms of the peace process and the Agreement it is sold as a resolution to the conflict. I think that is wrong, it is a major mistake – it's transforming a violent political conflict to one of political persuasion. Conflict won't be resolved, there has to be two winners.

What brings a community to the level that it feels it has to stop kids from going to school, and what brings parents to the level that they feel they have to insist on bringing their kids through that situation? Let's look at the problem, and start dealing with that problem.

Pete Shirlow Could I go back to an issue I talked about earlier on, about perpetrators and victims of conflict – "it wasn't me", type of thing. I think we have to be realistic, and the reason we have the type of society we have today is that people have been victims of violence, of sectarianism, of oppression, of an unfair state, of paramilitary violence, state violence... All of these things have created memories and experiences of living in this society. And the only thing which is ever going to heal this society is when people start to discuss that. It's okay for people here to say that Unionists wouldn't do this and Republicans won't do that. *Why* don't they do that? Because you are talking about different ideologies, different people, they understand violence in a different way. You know, I don't know anybody who is a Unionist who understands why the IRA did what they did; I don't know anyone who is a Republican who understands why people joined the police – unless in a negative way: they joined up because they were murderers, or bastards and wanted to do this to my community. But the actual reasons why we are the way we are is because we are different communities. We have different ideologies, different histories, different experiences, and that is where the genius of conflict resolution is, in enabling people to move away from those positions. And the problem is that in our society those positions are too ideologically strong. You're talking about different mentalities, but of the same political weight; there is no minority in this society any more.

We have different ideologies, different histories, different experiences, and that is where the genius of conflict resolution is, in enabling people to move away from those positions. And the problem is that in our society those positions are too ideologically strong... there is no minority in this society any more.

Male As Pete said earlier there was an agreement between the two governments and it was a fudge, and I think that it was a fudge and a management process until such times as we are mature enough to control ourselves and rule ourselves here, and until such time as there is a plebiscite and it goes to a United Ireland, or a Federal Ireland, or whatever it goes to after that. In the meantime it's a management process. But one thing that is not being tackled is sectarianism. I think people in government kind of thought: hopefully it'll go away. But it won't – it has to be faced up to. And what we should be thinking about is: how can communities play a role in this management process? I think the funders, who have put massive amounts of money in here, should have given it as a reward to communities which did start processes of cross-community activity, and this would hopefully have begun to undermine what the likes of the UDA are attempting to do.

Male I think the Good Friday Agreement is a sectarian solution to a sectarian society. And listening to some people talk tonight there seem to be some on the Nationalist/Republican side who think that the Unionists don't want it to work, and there's others on the Unionist side who think that Republicans are only in the whole process to make it collapse. And there's this sort of self-perpetuating hostility towards each other. I think we have moved away from a situation where we used to have a sectarian state to one now where we have a state in a very sectarian society, and the Good Friday Agreement merely reproduces those divisions. I think the Good Friday Agreement is a holding operation, what it is going to hold for I don't know. Another point: I don't think the peace process is under any threat of collapse, I think the peace process now defines this society and we will have a peace process in 50 years' time if society needs it to go on. It's just sad that there's people in it who support the process but do not support the peace.

Male If the Good Friday Agreement was about anything it was about an historical accommodation between Catholic Nationalism and Protestant Unionism. They thrashed out an accommodation where the representatives of Catholic

Nationalism and Protestant Unionism could meet in a commonly agreed forum, and start the process of working towards a tolerant and mature degree of politics. The question was posed: 'whatever happened to the peace process?', and I would agree with the more optimistic thoughts that were expressed tonight. There is no going back to the situation pre-April 1998. The Agreement wasn't a definitive document by any stretch of the imagination, it wasn't a panacea for all the ills of this society, but it was the start of the beginning of the end.

There is no going back to the situation pre-April 1998. The Agreement wasn't a definitive document by any stretch of the imagination, it wasn't a panacea for all the ills of this society, but it was the start of the beginning of the end.

Roy Garland It has been sold in the Unionist community as an imposed settlement. I heard a woman being interviewed on the street the other day and she said: oh, I don't see it as a peace process, but as an all-Ireland process. People have been sold the idea that the British government has an agenda to create an all-Ireland situation, and that the process was an imposed process to weaken the Union and lead in that direction. And the problem is that those who are against it seem more committed to undermining it than most of us are to making it work, and I think that has to change.

Barbara McCabe Thanks very much everybody for coming. I think an awful lot of people thought that Good Friday 1998 was the end, and they all went home to have a good night's sleep. And really that was only the start of the much more difficult task of trying to implement it and make it real. And I think that a lot of the things people have said tonight tells us that that discussion has yet to be tackled in a thorough way, to put meat on the bones of the Agreement and put it into practice. So thanks very much.

Postscript:

The day after the SICDP debate the two dissident members of David Trimble's Ulster Unionist Party voted against him at the Northern Ireland Assembly and managed to prevent his re-election as First Minister. However, a few days later two members of the Alliance Party temporarily 're-designated' themselves as 'Unionist' and this time the vote was successful.

Island Pamphlets

1. **Life on the Interface** Belfast 'peaceline' community groups confront common issues.
2. **Sacrifice on the Somme** Ulster's 'cross-community' sacrifice in the First World War.
3. **Ulster's Scottish Connection** Exploring the many links between Ulster and Scotland.
4. **Idle Hours** Belfast working-class poetry.
5. **Expecting the Future** A community play focusing on the effects of violence.
6. **Ulster's Shared Heritage** Exploring the cultural inheritance of the Ulster people.
7. **The Cruthin Controversy** A response to academic misrepresentation.
8. **Ulster's European Heritage** A celebration of Ulster's links with mainland Europe.
9. **Ulster's Protestant Working Class** A community exploration.
10. **The Battle of Moira** An adaptation of Sir Samuel Ferguson's epic poem *Congal.*
11. **Beyond the Fife and Drum** Belfast's Protestant Shankill Road debates the future.
12. **Belfast Community Economic Conference** Grassroots groups explore issues.
13. **A New Beginning** The Shankill Think Tank outlines its vision for the future.
14. **Reinforcing Powerlessness** Curtailing the voice of ordinary people.
15. **Ourselves Alone?** Belfast's Nationalist working class speak out.
16. **Hidden Frontiers** Addressing deep-rooted violent conflict in N. Ireland and Moldova.
17. **The Death of the Peace Process?** A survey of community perceptions.
18. **At the Crossroads?** Further explorations by the Shankill Think Tank.
19. **Conflict Resolution** The missing element in the Northern Ireland peace process.
20. **Young People Speak Out** An exploration of the needs of Nationalist youth in Belfast.
21. **Puppets No More** An exploration of socio-economic issues by Protestant East Belfast.
22. **Beyond King Billy?** East Belfast Protestants explore cultural & identity-related issues.
23. **Are we not part of this city too?** Protestant working-class alienation in Derry.
24. **Orangeism and the Twelfth** Report of a cultural debate held in Protestant East Belfast.
25. **Broadening Horizons** The impact of international travel on attitudes and perceptions.
26. **Before the 'Troubles'** Senior citizens from Belfast's Shankill Road reminisce.
27. **Seeds of Hope** A joint exploration by Republican and Loyalist ex-prisoners.
28. **Towards a Community Charter** An exploration by the Falls Think Tank.
29. **Restoring Relationships** A community exploration of restorative justice.
30. **Separated by Partition** An encounter between Protestants from Donegal and Belfast.
31. **Left in Limbo** The experience of Republican prisoners' children.
32. **A question of 'community relations'** Protestants discuss community relations issues.
33. **Beyond Friendship** An exploration of the value of cross-border exchanges.
34. **Catalysts for change** A Los Angeles / Northern Ireland / Moldovan exchange.
35. **Dunmurry Reflections** Reminiscences from the 'outskirts'.
36. **Community relations: an elusive concept** An exploration by community activists.
37. **Living in a mixed community** The experience of Ballynafeigh, Ormeau Road.
38. **Cross-border reflections on 1916** Report of a cross-border conference.
39. **The forgotten victims** The victims' group H.U.R.T. reveal the legacy of 'The Troubles'.
40. **The unequal victims** Discussion by members of Loughgall Truth and Justice Campaign.
41. **Citizenship in a modern society** Report of a public debate.
42. **Whatever happened to the Peace Process?** Report of a public debate.